History's
GREATEST RIVALS

ABRAHAM
LINCOLN
Vs.
JEFFERSON
DAVIS

PRESIDENTS OF A DIVIDED NATION

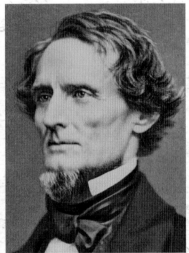

Ellis Roxburgh

Gareth Stevens
PUBLISHING

Please visit our website, **www.garethstevens.com**.
For a free color catalog of all our high-quality books,
call toll-free 1-800-542-2595 or fax 1-877-542-2596.

Library of Congress Cataloging-in-Publication Data

Roxburgh, Ellis.
 Abraham Lincoln vs. Jefferson Davis : presidents of a divided nation / Ellis Roxburgh.
    pages cm — (History's greatest rivals)
 Includes index.
 ISBN 978-1-4824-4219-9 (pbk.)
 ISBN 978-1-4824-4220-5 (6 pack)
 ISBN 978-1-4824-4221-2 (library binding)
 1. United States—History—Civil War, 1861-1865—Juvenile literature.
 2. Lincoln, Abraham, 1809-1865—Juvenile literature.
 3. Davis, Jefferson, 1808-1889—Juvenile literature. I. Title.
 E456.R69 2016
 973.7—dc23

                                  2015025566

Published in 2016 by
Gareth Stevens Publishing
111 East 14th Street, Suite 349
New York, NY 10003

© 2016 Brown Bear Books Ltd

For Brown Bear Books Ltd:
Editorial Director: Lindsey Lowe
Managing Editor: Tim Cooke
Children's Publisher: Anne O'Daly
Design Manager: Keith Davis
Designer: Lynne Lennon
Picture Manager: Sophie Mortimer

Picture Credits: T=Top, C=Center, B=Bottom, L=Left, R=Right. Front Cover: All images
Library of Congress. Harpers Weekly Archives: 21; Library of Congress: 4, 5, 10, 14, 18, 19, 26,
28, 29, 30, 33, 34, 35, 38, 39, 40 ; Missouri Historical Society: 9; National Portrait Gallery: 23;
NYPL: Pageant of America Collection 16; Palace of Versailles: 7; R.W. Norton Art Gallery:
27; Robert Hunt Library: 6, 12, 15, 22, 24, 25, 32; Shutterstock: 41, Everett Historical 11, 20, 31,
36, 37; Suffolk Record Office: 8; University of Kentucky: 13; Yale University: 17.

Brown Bear Books has made every attempt to contact the copyright holder. If anyone
has any information please contact licensing@brownbearbooks.co.uk

Manufactured in the United States of America

CPSIA compliance information: Batch #CW16GS. For further information contact
Gareth Stevens, New York, New York at 1-800-542-2595.

CONTENTS

AT ODDS

ABRAHAM LINCOLN Vs. JEFFERSON DAVIS

The president who led the Union to victory in the Civil War (1861–1865) was Abraham Lincoln (1809–1865). His dedication to preserving the Union has been admired ever since.

* Lincoln came from a poor family. He only spent a year in school and was largely self-educated.

* Before he became president, Lincoln had served just a single term in Congress.

* Lincoln never actively served in the military and never owned slaves.

* Lincoln worked well with people.

Jefferson Davis (1808–1889) did not believe the Southern states should leave the Union. He also didn't want to become president of the Confederacy. His leadership during the war has been widely criticized.

* Davis came from a wealthy family. He inherited a large plantation and owned more than 100 slaves.

* Before he became president, Davis had 15 years' political experience.

* Davis was also an experienced military man who served in the Mexican War (1846–1848).

* He was known for his inflexibility and unwillingness to change his mind under any circumstances.

CONTEXT

The circumstances that led to the Civil War and the clash between Abraham Lincoln and Jefferson Davis had their roots in the early settlement of America.

European settlers began to bring African slaves to America in the middle of the 16th century. Many Americans later came to oppose slavery, however. On January 1, 1808, the African slave trade was outlawed. But while this meant that no more slaves could be imported, slavery itself was still legal in parts of the United States. The country was split over the issue. In the North, most states did not allow slavery. However, in the South, the economy was based on

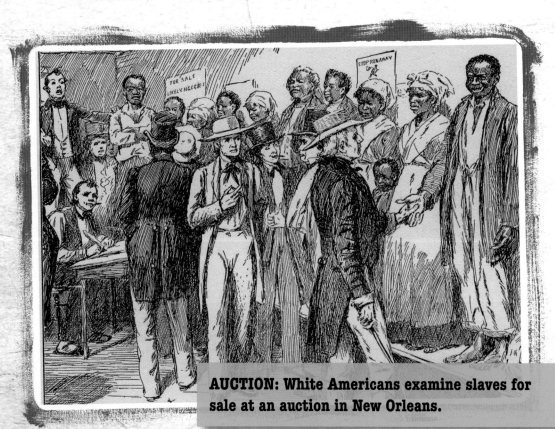

AUCTION: White Americans examine slaves for sale at an auction in New Orleans.

ABOLITION: Slaves celebrate the abolition of slavery in the French empire in 1848.

plantations that grew cotton, tobacco, and other crops. The plantations relied on slaves. The invention of the cotton gin in 1793 had mechanized the cotton industry. Slaves were needed to pick cotton more quickly to keep the machines running. Many Northerners argued that no human should be able to own another. Southerners argued that slavery benefited both the slaves and their owners.

Changing Developments

At the start of the 19th century, the country was fairly evenly balanced between slave states

> **“ Fortunately for the South, she found a race inferior to her own. We use them for our purpose, and call them slaves. ”**
>
> **James Henry Hammond, Governor of South Carolina, 1858**

and free, or non-slave, states. The situation changed, however, as the country expanded in the first half of the century. In 1803, the United States bought a huge area of the West from France in the Louisiana Purchase. As this new land was divided into states and territories, the government had to decide whether or not to allow slavery there. In 1820, it created an imaginary line dividing the country. New states south of the line would allow slavery; those to the north would not. The arrangement was intended to maintain the balance between free and slave states.

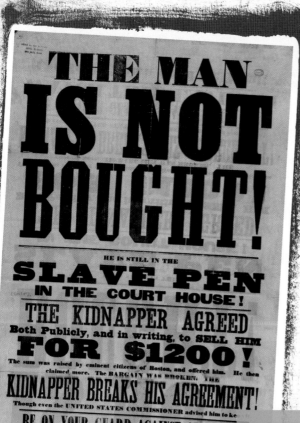

When Kansas and Nebraska became territories of the Union in 1854, however, Congress decided to allow settlers to decide for themselves whether to allow slavery. Kansas voted to become a slave state, even though it was north of the line. The balance of slave and free states had been destroyed.

POSTER: This poster was printed by Bostonians trying to buy a slave his freedom.

SCOTT: Dred Scott wanted to be freed because he had lived in a free state for four years.

Growing Pressure

The forces against slavery were growing. European countries had banned slavery in the early 19th century. Within the United States, a powerful movement also pressed for its abolition. In 1857 a slave named Dred Scott asked the Supreme Court to free him on the grounds that he had lived in the free state of Missouri for four years and had married a free black woman. At the time, Scott was living in Louisiana, which was a slave state. The court refused. Abolitionists were outraged. Politicians opposed to slavery began to give up the idea of balance and compromise. They would have to make a stand.

> ❝ A crime against nature, from which the soul recoils, and which language refuses to describe. ❞

Massachusetts senator Charles Sumner describes the adoption of slavery in Kansas, 1854

ABRAHAM LINCOLN

From his humble beginnings, few would have thought Abraham Lincoln would become one of the greatest of all American presidents.

Lincoln was born in a Kentucky log cabin on February 12, 1809. His parents were Baptists who opposed slavery, a view which influenced Lincoln's whole life. His mother died when he was nine years old, and his father remarried. The family moved to Indiana and then to Illinois. Lincoln went to school for a year, but he gave up his education to earn money. He worked as a clerk in a general store. He spent his spare time reading and teaching himself law and history.

PORTRAIT: Observers said that Lincoln often looked sad, but he was passionate when he spoke.

KENTUCKY: Abraham Lincoln was born in this modest log cabin in Kentucky.

A Political Career

Lincoln became a successful lawyer and began a career in politics. In 1834, he won a seat in the state legislature, where he served until 1842. In 1846, Lincoln won a seat in the US Congress. He spent two years in Congress before returning to his law practice. In 1858, he ran against Stephen A. Douglas to become a US senator. The two men held seven debates in which Lincoln argued strongly against slavery. Although Lincoln lost the election, the debates brought him to national attention. He won the Republican Party nomination for president two years later, and in November 1860 became president of the United States.

> " In your hands, my dissatisfied fellow countrymen, and not in mine, is the momentous issue of civil war. "

Abraham Lincoln addresses southerners, inauguration speech, March 4, 1861

JEFFERSON DAVIS

Jefferson Davis seemed to have the skills and military and political experience to make a great president, but in practice he was not a success.

Jefferson Davis was born into a wealthy Kentucky family on June 3, 1808. He grew up on cotton plantations owned by his older brother, Joseph, in Louisiana and Mississippi. After going to boarding school, Davis was accepted into the US Military Academy in West Point in 1824. He served in the US Army from 1828 to 1835, before leaving to marry the colonel's daughter, Sarah Knox Taylor. They settled down on a plantation given to him by his brother Joseph. Sarah died from malaria only a few months later.

OFFICER: Davis was injured in the Mexican War, but was recognized for his bravery in action.

Political Career

Davis later returned to the army to serve with success as a colonel in the Mexican War. However, between his

HOME: Jefferson Davis was born in a four-room home built by his father in Fairview, Kentucky.

periods in the army, Davis had entered politics as a Democrat. He was elected to the House of Representatives in 1845, but resigned the following year to fight in the Mexican War. He was injured during the conflict. After the war ended, Davis returned to the Senate and became Secretary of War in 1853. He enlarged the size of the army and strengthened coastal defenses. As divisions over slavery seemed to drive the country toward civil war, Davis argued in both the North and the South that the two factions should come to an agreement.

> **An appeal to arms should be the last resort, and only by national rights or national honor can it be justified.**
>
> Jefferson Davis, February 6, 1846

ALLIES OF THE UNION

President Lincoln surrounded himself with advisors who would challenge his ideas. He believed this was the best way to reach the right decisions.

Lincoln's cabinet included political opponents, such as William H. Seward, who had been Lincoln's rival for the Republican presidential nomination in 1860. Lincoln made Seward secretary of state. Seward had far more political experience, but Lincoln was not afraid to overrule him. However, Seward came to respect Lincoln's decisions.

Military Commanders

One of Lincoln's gifts was to recognize potential in other people. In 1864, three years after the start of the war, he made Ulysses S. Grant commander of all the Union armies. There was nothing to suggest

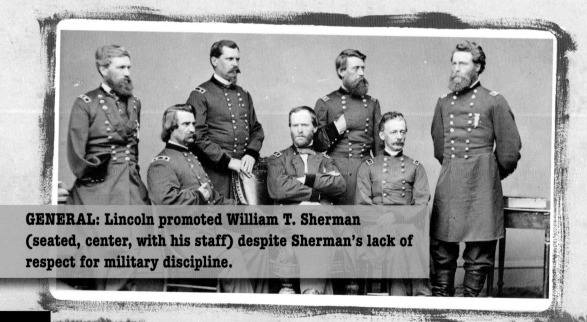

GENERAL: Lincoln promoted William T. Sherman (seated, center, with his staff) despite Sherman's lack of respect for military discipline.

WIFE: Mary Todd Lincoln was criticized by some people in Washington, D.C., for her coarse "Western" manners.

Grant would become an outstanding commander, but Lincoln's faith in Grant was repaid by success. Grant's deputy, William T. Sherman, also seemed an unlikely officer. He had little time for regulations. However, his fighting skill proved Lincoln's judgment right again.

Mary Todd Lincoln

Lincoln had married Mary Todd in 1842. They had four sons, although two died as children. Mary came from a slave-owning family in Kentucky, and some of her relatives fought on the side of the Confederacy. She was a strong supporter of her husband's policies, however. She tried to keep life at the White House as normal as possible during the war.

> " **Grant is my man and I am his the rest of the war.** "

Lincoln on Ulysses S. Grant, July 5, 1863

RELUCTANT REBELS

Unlike Lincoln, Jefferson Davis did not like to take advice from others. Many of his friends opposed his views about the war.

Davis was president of the Confederacy. However, some of his closest allies supported the Union. They included his second wife, Varina Howell Davis. They had married in 1845. Varina was in favor of slavery but did not want the South to leave the Union. She did not enjoy her time as First Lady of the Confederacy. Alexander Stephens served as vice president to Davis. He never gave up his support for the Union, and spent four years criticizing the Southern war effort. Davis ignored his advice. He also ignored John C. Breckinridge, his secretary of war, who urged Davis to surrender.

DOUBT: Varina Davis was open about her belief that her husband was not suited for politics.

VICE PRESIDENT: Alexander Stephens (right) argued that black Americans were naturally suited to be slaves.

Military Genius

In 1862, in one of the key moments of his presidency, Davis replaced the wounded Joseph Johnston with Robert E. Lee as commander of the Army of Northern Virginia. Most of the Confederate victories that followed were due to Lee's tactical brilliance. But despite having a good relationship with Davis, Lee was not allowed to control Confederate strategy. Davis had the final say in all military matters.

> **" He has a way of taking for granted that everybody agrees with him when he expresses an opinion. "**

Varina Howell Davis describes her first meeting with Davis, 1843

LINES ARE DRAWN

One issue dominated the 1860 presidential election. Would the United States allow slavery to continue?

Lincoln had joined the new Republican Party when it formed. It was opposed to slavery. To everyone's surprise (including Lincoln's own), Lincoln became the party's presidential candidate early in 1860. The opposing Democratic Party was split into Northern and Southern groups that argued between themselves. It always seemed likely the Republicans would win the election. The Southern Democrats were already planning to leave the Union before Lincoln won the election on November 4, 1860.

PRESIDENT: Crowds gather for the inauguration of Abraham Lincoln in Washington, D.C., on March 4, 1861.

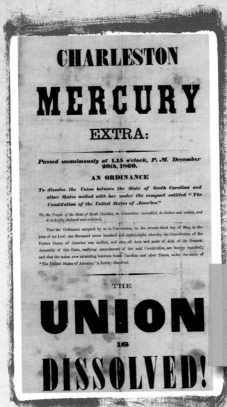

SECESSION: A Charleston newspaper announces South Carolina's vote to leave the Union on December 20, 1860.

The Secession Crisis

Many people in both the North and the South viewed Lincoln's victory with dismay because it meant the inevitable breakup of the United States. Just over a month after the election, on December 20, 1860, South Carolina became the first state to leave the Union. Six more states quickly seceded: Mississippi, Florida, Alabama, Georgia, Louisiana, and Texas. When Lincoln was inaugurated on March 4, 1861, he became president of a country that was rapidly shrinking.

> " There is an enmity between the Northern and Southern people that is deep and enduring, and you never can eradicate it, never! "
>
> **Senator Alfred Iverson of Georgia, December 4, 1860**

A NEW COUNTRY

Although Jefferson Davis was not in favor of secession, his military and political experience made him an obvious leader for the South.

After Mississippi seceded in January 1861, Davis believed he had no choice but to resign from the US Senate and support the South. He made a farewell speech to the Senate on January 21, 1861, and returned to his plantation, Brierfield, Mississippi. He still hoped the Union would remain intact. However, as more states seceded it became clear war was coming. With his military experience, Davis assumed that he would be called upon to lead Mississippi's armed forces. He awaited a call from the new government.

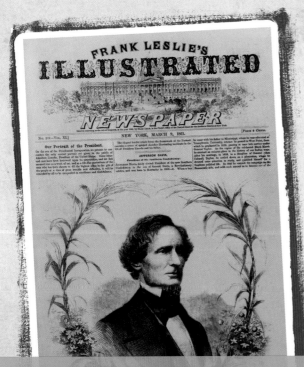

LEADER: Jefferson was chosen as president for his military and political experience.

Unexpected Call

On February 10, 1861, Davis was in his garden when he received a telegram from Montgomery, Alabama. A constitutional convention was meeting there to decide the laws for a new country: the Confederate States of America. The representatives from the states had unanimously

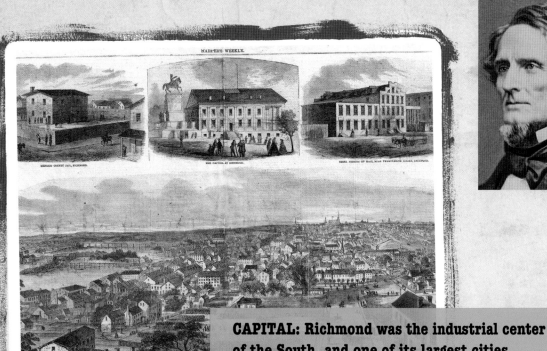

CAPITAL: Richmond was the industrial center of the South, and one of its largest cities.

chosen Davis to be the first president. Jefferson was reluctant to accept the role, but he believed it was his duty. Just eight days later, he was sworn in as Confederate president in Montgomery. Three years later, the Confederates moved their capital from Montgomery to Richmond, Virginia, just 100 miles (160 km) south of Washington, D.C. Northern troops would advance on Richmond twice during the coming war.

> **" I worked day and night for twelve years to prevent the war, but I could not. "**

Jefferson Davis on the coming of war, 1865

The Northern Enemy

Although Davis had not wanted the Union to split, he was totally committed to the cause of the Confederacy and set out to demonize

Northerners as a way to justify separation from the Union. This behavior was in direct contrast to Abraham Lincoln. Throughout the war, Lincoln maintained an attitude he later described as "malice toward none."

A Tricky Problem

As soon as he became president, Davis set up a commission to negotiate with the federal government over issues that might complicate the South's departure from the Union. Lincoln's secretary of state, William H. Seward, negotiated on behalf of the Union. One of the trickiest issues was what to do with federal forts and lighthouses that were now within Confederate

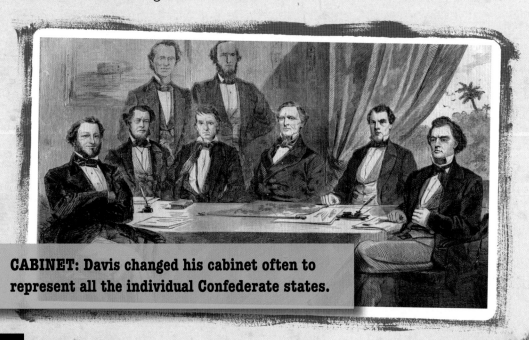

CABINET: Davis changed his cabinet often to represent all the individual Confederate states.

territory. Lincoln, however, insisted that any federal facilities remained federal property, and that he was entitled to keep them manned by Union troops. The debate soon came to focus on Charleston, South Carolina. Charleston Harbor was guarded by a network of defenses, including Fort Moultrie and Fort Sumter.

Davis prepared for war. He sent General Pierre G. T. Beauregard to take command of the Confederate troops in Charleston. Beauregard began to strengthen the defenses and artillery positions around the harbor where the Union fortifications lay.

COMMANDER: General Pierre Gustave Toutant Beauregard was the first senior general in the Confederate army.

FORT SUMTER

The attention of both presidents Lincoln and Davis came to focus on federal-held Fort Sumter in Charleston Harbor, South Carolina.

Shortly after South Carolina announced its secession, Union commander Major Robert Anderson moved his men from Fort Moultrie, near the mouth of Charleston Harbor, to Fort Sumter. Fort Sumter lay on an island in the middle of the harbor, so he thought it would be easier to defend. When Anderson requested supplies, Lincoln faced a dilemma. During his negotiations with the Confederates, William H. Seward had suggested that the Union might evacuate the fort. But Lincoln decided to resupply the fort instead as a signal that he intended to maintain a federal presence

FORT: Anderson commanded 85 men in Fort Sumter; none were killed in the bombardment.

ARTILLERY: Confederate cannons along the shore of Charleston Harbor open fire on Fort Sumter.

in South Carolina. Davis and his cabinet had to decide how to react. Lincoln insisted that resupplying the troops at Fort Sumter was not an aggressive act. Davis decided that he did not agree.

Confederate Response

General Beauregard had his artillery positioned around the harbor ready to fire on the fort. Davis ordered him to ask for Anderson's surrender. When Anderson refused to surrender, the Confederate artillery opened fire early on the morning of April 12, 1861. After 34 hours of bombardment, Anderson surrendered the fort. The Civil War had started.

> **If we never meet in this world again, God grant that we may meet in the next.**
>
> Major Robert Anderson to Confederate representatives, April 11, 1861

OPPOSING PLANS

Lincoln and Davis were both in charge of military strategy for their respective sides. Of the two, Davis had more military experience.

Despite the loss of Fort Sumter, Lincoln believed the North would win the war. It had more men, more resources, and more industry than the South; it had more ships and more railroads for transportation and supplies. Unlike Davis, Lincoln also had the benefit of an established army. When the war started Lincoln studied everything he could about military strategy. He and his generals decided their best option was to starve the Confederates into submission. They planned to set up a blockade to prevent food or other supplies from reaching the South.

SNAKE: The Union intended its blockade to squeeze the South like a constricting snake.

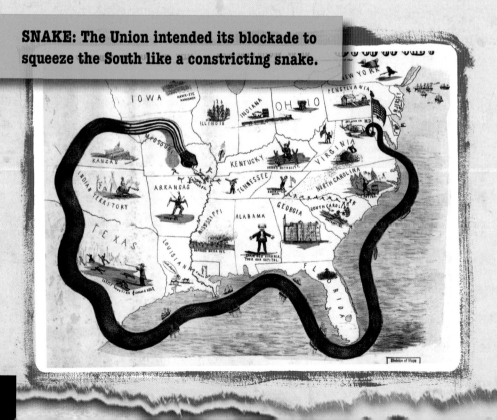

RIDER: Jefferson Davis was a skilled horseman, thanks partly to his time served as an army officer.

A Defensive Strategy

Unlike Lincoln, Davis had to build an army from scratch. He had to rely on Confederate soldiers supplying their own weapons and horses. Davis understood the dangers of being drawn into a long defensive war. The longer the war went on, the more the Union's advantage in men and resources would give it the edge. Davis decided the Confederacy's best strategy would be to invade the North in the hopes of achieving a quick, decisive victory.

> " Determine that the thing can and shall be done, and then find the way. "
>
> **Abraham Lincoln, June 20, 1848**

SENIOR GENERALS

Lincoln and Davis differed in the way they hired their generals. Lincoln tried to choose the best man for the job. Davis preferred to appoint friends.

GENERAL: Grant was said to drink too much, but Lincoln trusted him.

Throughout the war, Lincoln replaced generals he thought were doing badly. When the Union lost the first battle of the war at Bull Run (Manassas) on July 21, 1861, Lincoln fired the commander, General Irvin McDowell. When Lincoln's general-in-chief, George B. McClellan, did not seem to want to commit his army to big battles, Lincoln removed him in 1862. His smartest move was to appoint Ulysses S. Grant as commander of all the Union armies in March 1864. Lincoln had promoted Grant regularly over the previous two years. He liked Grant's aggressive tactics.

Loyalty to Friends

Unlike Lincoln, Jefferson Davis made his friends generals. He also often meddled in their strategies. One of his biggest mistakes was to appoint a former classmate from West Point, Leonidas Polk, as a

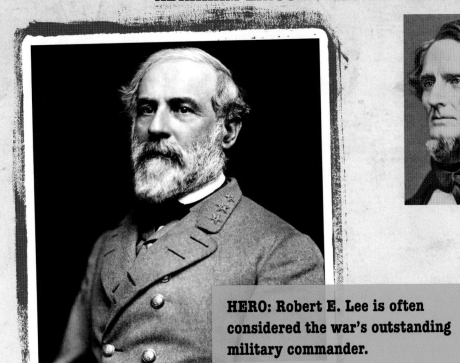

HERO: Robert E. Lee is often considered the war's outstanding military commander.

general. Polk was put in command of an area between the Mississippi and Tennessee Rivers, even though he had no military experience. Polk sent troops to occupy Columbus, Kentucky. Kentucky had been neutral in the war. Polk's decision made it decide to side with the Union.

> " If General McClellan isn't going to use his army, I'd like to borrow it for a time. "
>
> **Abraham Lincoln commenting on McClellan's reluctance to fight, 1862**

One of Davis's great successes came when he hired someone who was not a friend. He put General Robert E. Lee in charge of the Army of Northern Virginia. Lee was a master tactician and his strategy won many battles against much larger Union forces.

FREEING THE SLAVES

Lincoln had maintained that the war was not about slavery but about the preservation of the Union. That changed on January 1, 1863.

One of Jefferson Davis's most important war aims was to win the support of France and Britain. If the European countries recognized the Confederacy as a country in its own right, they would be able to send it supplies. They could not help if the Union convinced them that the South was merely a region in rebellion. Davis was hopeful of receiving their backing because Britain, in particular, relied heavily on importing cotton from the South. In Europe, the French and British decided to wait until the outcome of the war became clearer.

WRITING: Lincoln wrote the Emancipation Proclamation in July 1862, but waited for the best time to publish it.

A War About Slavery

In September 1862 Confederate troops led by Robert E. Lee invaded the North. The invasion was stopped at the Battle of Antietam in Maryland on September 17, and Lee's army withdrew. Five days later, Lincoln issued his Emancipation Proclamation. He announced that on January 1, 1863, all slaves in the rebellious states would be freed.

> **" What I do about slavery, and the colored race, I do because I believe it helps to save the Union. "**
>
> Abraham Lincoln, August 22, 1862

This was the turning point in the war. What began as a struggle to preserve the Union became a struggle for freedom. France and Britain would not support a fight to preserve slavery. Davis had lost any hope of any foreign support.

THE FREEDMEN

Although Lincoln had been persuaded to allow African Americans to serve in the Union Army, Davis banned freed slaves from military service.

At the start of the war, Lincoln worried that if he allowed black soldiers to serve it would convince Union slave states on the border to join the Confederacy. As the war went on, however, he changed his mind. The Union Army needed men. After the Emancipation Proclamation in 1863, black soldiers were free to enlist. A black regiment, the 54th Massachusetts Regiment, was created. All its officers were white. Within other regiments, however, black soldiers were often treated badly and subjected to racism by other soldiers. Davis also threatened that black Union soldiers caught in the South would be enslaved or executed.

RECRUITS: These two African American brothers served in the Union armies.

ASSAULT: The 54th
Massachusetts Regiment storm
Fort Wagner in July 1863.

A Late Change of Mind

The Confederate Army banned slaves from military service although
it badly needed reinforcements. Despite this, it was only in March
1865 that Davis allowed black slaves to join up. By then, the South
was facing defeat. Union armies threatened the capital at Richmond
and were marching through the South. The change of mind came too
late to make a difference to the Confederate cause.

> " A measure by which several millions of
> human beings of an inferior race, peaceful
> and contented laborers in their sphere, are
> doomed to extermination. "

Jefferson Davis on the Emancipation Proclamation,
January 12, 1863

FALL OF RICHMOND

After a siege lasting nine months, the Confederate capital at Richmond fell to the Union Army of Ulysses S. Grant in April 1865.

At the start of April, General Robert E. Lee was commanding a desperate defense of Richmond. He was based in Petersburg, Virginia, guarding the approach to the capital. By late March, however, he realized that his weak troops could not hold out much longer. On March 25, he made one last attempt to break through Union defenses. The attempt failed, with the loss of 4,800 men. The Union troops passed Petersburg and began their final attack on Richmond.

EVACUATION: Citizens flee from Richmond across the James River on April 2, 1865.

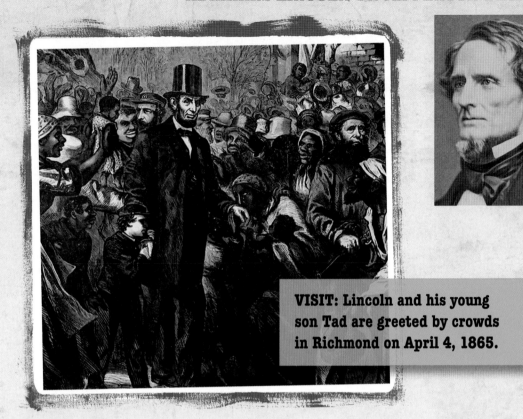

VISIT: Lincoln and his young son Tad are greeted by crowds in Richmond on April 4, 1865.

The War Is Over

On April 2, 1865, the Union bombardment of Richmond began. Lee told Davis to prepare to leave. Davis had already sent his family out of the city. Davis delayed his own departure, still hoping Lee would manage to save Richmond. At 11:30 p.m., Davis and his cabinet boarded a train for Danville, Virginia, which was to be the new Confederate capital. Two days later, Abraham Lincoln arrived in Richmond. He toured the city and sat at Davis's desk in the Confederate president's mansion. Meanwhile, Lee tried to get his army to safety but was trapped by Ulysses S. Grant. Lee surrendered at Appomattox Courthouse on April 9, 1865. The Civil War was over.

> **I advise that all preparation be made for leaving Richmond tonight.**

Robert E. Lee writes to Jefferson Davis, April 2, 1865

ASSASSINATION

Lincoln began planning for the recovery of the nation, but he would never see it. Within a week of the Confederate surrender, he was shot dead.

After the surrender at Appomattox, Lincoln prepared plans to reunite the nation. He did not want to make the South suffer further. Lincoln proposed that if 10 percent of the population of a Southern state would swear allegiance to the United States, that state would be readmitted into the Union. Congress tried to insist that 50 percent of the population should swear the oath, but Lincoln would not approve the bill. However, Lincoln would not live to see his dream of the nation's reconciliation come to pass.

ESCAPE: John Wilkes Booth jumps to the stage to escape after shooting Lincoln in his box at the theater.

CEREMONY: Lincoln's body lies in state in City Hall, New York.

Assassination of the President

On the night of April 14, 1865, Lincoln and his wife went to Ford's Theater in Washington, D.C. As they watched the play, John Wilkes Booth, a famous actor and Confederate supporter, shot Lincoln in the head. Lincoln died the following day. His death stunned the country. He received the grandest funeral ever given to a president.

> " With malice toward none, with charity for all ... Let us strive to ... bind up the nation's wounds. "

Abraham Lincoln, second inauguration address,
March 4, 1865

AFTER THE WAR

At the end of the war Jefferson Davis was captured. He has since often been dismissed as a failure and coward.

Although Jefferson Davis had fled Richmond for Danville, Virginia, he tried to keep his generals fighting. Even after Robert E. Lee had surrendered, Davis could not accept that the war was lost. He fled Virginia, planning to escape to Europe. He hoped a sympathetic country might take him in and allow him to form a government in exile. Before he could get away, however, Davis was captured by Union forces in Georgia on May 10, 1865. According to Northern newspapers, Davis was in women's clothing to try to escape capture.

Davis was imprisoned for two years for treason. He was never tried, however. Northerners feared a trial might reopen old wounds. They also worried that a trial might allow Davis publicity to argue that the Confederacy had been a legal country.

MUSIC: This song was published to poke fun at the rumor that Jefferson tried to escape dressed as a woman.

"JEFF'S DOUBLE QUICK."

FUNERAL: Davis died in New Orleans on December 6, 1889.

After the War

Davis was released from prison in 1867 and worked in an insurance company. In 1877 he inherited a Mississippi plantation from a wealthy supporter. Although he wrote his memoirs, Davis kept his views of the war private and remained largely out of public life until in 1881 he published his book, *The Rise and Fall of the Confederate Government*. He died on December 6, 1889.

> " The contest is not over, the strife is not ended. It has only entered upon a new and enlarged arena. "

Jefferson Davis, speech to the Mississippi legislature, 1881

AFTERMATH

After the death of Lincoln it fell to Vice President Andrew Johnson, a Southerner, to guide the United States through Reconstruction.

FREEDMEN: Former slaves prepare to leave their plantation in South Carolina.

Reconstruction lasted until 1877. Vice President Andrew Johnson, who became president on Lincoln's death, was a Southerner. He pardoned thousands of former Confederates who had led the South's rebellion in 1861. He also abandoned Lincoln's plan to give the vote to some Freedmen, as former slaves were known. Johnson also clashed with the US Congress after the Southern states introduced the "Black Codes" in 1865 and 1866. These laws restricted the ability of Freedmen to own land or work as free laborers and denied them civil and political rights.

MONUMENT: The Lincoln Memorial in Washington, D.C., commemorates Lincoln's role in the nation's history.

Difficult Freedom

Against Johnson's will, Congress sent the US Army to protect the rights of former slaves in the South. It also set up the Freedmen's Bureau to help the former slaves. Life for African Americans was still difficult. Many freedmen went back to work on the plantations, even though the pay was poor. Little seemed to have changed in the South. The government withdrew troops from the South in 1877, marking the end of Reconstruction. African Americans had gained their freedom, but their lives were still inferior to those of most white Americans.

> " I am sworn to uphold the Constitution as Andy Johnson understands it and interprets it. "
>
> **Andrew Johnson, 1866**

JUDGMENT

ABRAHAM LINCOLN **Vs.** JEFFERSON DAVIS

Abraham Lincoln's reputation remains high. He is revered as the man who saved the Union and freed the slaves, but who also paid for his achievements with his life.

* Lincoln did not want war to come, but he understood that the question of slavery made it unavoidable.

* Lincoln believed that slavery was morally wrong, but he argued that the war was about saving the Union, not about slavery.

* Lincoln waited to issue the Emancipation Proclamation until the North was in a strong military position.

* Lincoln made plans to reunite the country without being unnecessarily harsh on the South.

Jefferson Davis did not choose to become Confederate president. After he was appointed, he always faced an uphill task to win the war, given the greater resources of the North.

* **Davis had numerous personal failings. His inflexibility and inability to take advice made winning the war even more difficult than it already was.**

* **Davis struggled to keep up morale in the South as the Union blockade took effect.**

* **The international support Davis hoped for became impossible after Lincoln issued the Emancipation Proclamation.**

TIMELINE

Abraham Lincoln and Jefferson Davis each believed it was his duty to take on leadership of a cause. For Lincoln the cause was saving the Union; for Davis, it was preserving the rights of the states.

New President
In November, the antislavery Republican candidate Abraham Lincoln is elected president of the United States.

Farewell Speech
On January 21, Jefferson Davis makes his last speech to the US Senate, explaining that he must be loyal to his home state.

First Shots
Early on April 12, Confederate forces in Charleston open fire on Fort Sumter, which Lincoln has refused to evacuate. The Civil War begins.

1860

1861

1862

Union Divided
On December 20, South Carolina becomes the first state to leave the Union. It is followed by six more before February 1861.

New President
On February 9, Jefferson Davis becomes president of the Confederate States of America; his position is confirmed by an election in November.

Military Leader
In June, Davis appoints Robert E. Lee to lead the Army of Northern Virginia; he wants Lee to lead an invasion of the North to try to achieve a rapid victory.

Momentous Battle
On September 22, five days after Union forces halt Lee in the Battle of Antietam, Lincoln issues the Emancipation Proclamation, offering to free slaves in the South.

Fighting Man
Having steadily promoted General Ulysses S. Grant over the previous year, on March 12 Abraham Lincoln makes him commander in chief of all the Union armies.

Death of Lincoln
On April 14, Lincoln is at the theater with his wife when he is shot by Confederate supporter John Wilkes Booth; Lincoln dies the next day.

1863   **1864**   **1865**   **1889**

Freedom!
On January 1, the Emancipation Proclamation comes into effect; the conflict is now a war against slavery.

Fall of Richmond
On April 2, Davis flees from Richmond; Lee surrenders to Grant a week later. Davis is captured while trying to escape on May 10 and is held in jail for two years.

Death of Davis
Having recently completed his book *A Short History of the Confederate States of America*, Davis dies on December 8, 1889.

GLOSSARY

abolition The action of ending a practice, such as slavery.

allegiance Loyalty to a person or a cause.

artillery Big, powerful guns, such as cannons.

assassination A murder carried out for political reasons.

blockade The act of sealing off a place to prevent goods from entering or leaving.

bombardment A continuous attack with bombs and shells.

cabinet The group of senior ministers who control the policy of a government.

compromise A solution to a dispute in which each side makes concessions to the other.

Confederacy The Confederate States of America, created by the Southern states that left the Union.

Congress The body that creates laws in the United States; it consists of the Senate and the House of Representatives.

cotton gin A machine for separating cotton from its seeds.

demonize Portray as wicked and inhuman.

dilemma A difficult choice that has to be made between two alternatives.

emancipation The act of setting someone free from slavery.

enmity A feeling of hostility or hatred.

evacuate To move from a place of danger to a place of safety.

exile The state of being barred from one's home country.

factions Groups within an organization that disagree with one another.

federal Relating to the central government of the Union rather than the governments of its member states.

neutral Not taking sides in a conflict.

plantation A large agricultural estate growing crops such as cotton or tobacco.

proclamation An official declaration that has the force of a law.

Reconstruction The period from 1865 to 1877 when the Southern states were controlled directly by the federal government.

secede To formally withdraw from a union or alliance.

secession The act of seceding, or leaving a union or alliance.

Senate The small upper assembly in the US Congress.

siege A military action in which a place is surrounded in order to force it to surrender.

strategy A plan designed to achieve a large-scale or long-term goal.

tactical Related to tactics, or plans designed to achieve a specific, short-term goal.

treason The crime of trying to overthrow a monarch or government.

Union The name given to the Northern states that remained in the United States during the Civil War.

FOR FURTHER INFORMATION

Books

Aretha, David A. *Jefferson Davis* (Leaders of the Civil War Era). Chelsea House Publishers, 2009.

Baxter, Roberta. *The Southern Home Front of the Civil War*. Heinemann Library, 2011.

Benoit, Peter. *Abraham Lincoln* (True Books: Civil War). Scholastic, 2011.

Pascal, Janet. *Who Was Abraham Lincoln?* (Who Was?). Turtleback, 2008.

Press, David Paul. *Abraham Lincoln: The Great Emancipator* (Voices for Freedom). Crabtree Publishing Company, 2013.

Wagner, Heather Lehr. *The Outbreak of the Civil War: A Nation Tears Apart* (Milestones in American History). Chelsea House Publishers, 2009.

Websites

http://amhistory.si.edu/militaryhistory/printable/section.asp?id=5
Printable guide to the Civil War from the Smithsonian Institution.

http://www.history.com/topics/american-civil-war/jefferson-davis
History.com page about Jefferson Davis, with videos and links.

https://www.whitehouse.gov/1600/presidents/abrahamlincoln
Biography of Abraham Lincoln from the White House, Washington, D.C.

http://millercenter.org/president/lincoln
Page about Lincoln from the University of Virginia, with links to discussions of all aspects of his administration.

http://www.ducksters.com/history/civilwartimeline.php
Ducksters.com timeline of the Civil War, with many links to specific pages.

http://www.historyplace.com/civilwar/
History Place guide to the Civil War.

INDEX